Why
GENESIS
Matters

Why GENESIS Matters

CHRISTIAN DOCTRINE AND THE CREATION ACCOUNT

JASON LISLE

INSTITUTE FOR
CREATION
RESEARCH

Dallas, Texas
www.icr.org

WHY GENESIS MATTERS

by Jason Lisle, Ph.D.

All Scripture quotations are from the New King James Version.

ISBN: 978-1-935587-11-8
Library of Congress Catalog Number: 2012939463

Please visit our website for other books and resources: www.icr.org

Printed in the United States of America.

TABLE OF CONTENTS

FOREWORD

The world is beginning to reap the harvest of millennia of polytheistic and pantheistic religions, now concentrated in a well-established evolutionary worldview that dominates global thinking. Evolutionary processes are seen as directed by the Consciousness (deity implied) of the universe, the random interplay of blind forces, or the mysterious management of Natural Selection—however presented, all things have evolved out of the primeval chaos of the eternal essence of whatever makes up the universe.

The message of the Bible is diametrically different. Does that matter?

Although there are varied logical systems, scientific philosophies, and theological interpretations that vie for our souls, they all attempt to answer the age-old question: "What is man?" Scrape away all the technical jargon and liturgical mysteries, and they all boil down to an attempt to define who or what we are and how we got here. And since that study depends on the presuppositions one holds to be true (no human was around to observe what happened when the universe began), then the answers produced by such studies impact the entirety of knowledge—the study of origins *does* matter!

Would it matter if God were real and the creation really happened like He said?

"In the beginning God created the heavens and the earth" (Genesis 1:1).

This astounding claim, unique in all literature, has enormous implications. The Bible insists that Jesus Christ was the Creator (John 1:1-3; Colossians 1:16; Hebrews 1:2). If that is true, then "Nor is there salvation in any other, for there is no other name under heaven given among men, by which we must be saved" (Acts 4:12).

But apart from the claim that one's eternal destiny is directly tied to the belief in the creation account and the Creator who made everything and will judge all men, all of science (knowledge) is affected. Not only must we understand that the universe and all that is in it were *created*, but we must know that everything has been *designed* by the omnipotent and omniscient God and has a purpose for being. Those foundational matters do matter!

"So God created...every living thing that moves" (Genesis 1:21).

The Bible's message is simple: The One who is life, created life (John 1:4). That concept is profound. Life is unique. Life itself reflects the nature of the Creator Himself. Although death is now the last enemy because of man's rebellion against his Creator, life is still most precious. Life is miraculous. Life is wonderful. Life is both mysterious and majestic. Life is to be valued, protected, and conserved. One's view of life matters—a lot!

"So God created man in His own image; in the image of God He created him; male and female He created them" (Genesis 1:27).

Three times God insists that man was *created*. Man is not some higher order of ape. Man bears the image of the Creator. You and I are unique in all of creation. We are not the product of ages of random atomic interplay. The omnipotent and omniscient Creator *personally* designed us (Genesis 1:27; Psalm 94:9; Psalm 139:14; Isaiah 44:24). Evolutionary science vehemently denies the supernatural—especially the thought that God promises eternal life to those who receive His gift of salvation. Our view of life *matters*.

Dr. Jason Lisle has written a powerful defense for the importance of a historical Genesis. Many in the evangelical world have capitulated to various hybrids of the creation message and have either relegated Genesis to the murky waters of myth and allegory or tossed it into the trash can of irrelevance. Dr. Lisle makes a clear case—if you trash Genesis, you trash the gospel. Genesis does matter!

Henry M. Morris III, D.Min.
Institute for Creation Research
Dallas, Texas

INTRODUCTION

D oes the creation versus evolution debate matter today? Perhaps you have heard people say, "With all the problems in today's world, we really shouldn't bother arguing about how it all began. We need to be concerned about the future, not the past."

Our world faces enormous problems—violence, war, crime, disease, famine, economic collapse, natural disasters, and much more. We're seeing attacks on the sanctity of human life and attempts to redefine marriage. We have witnessed a decline in Christian values worldwide, but it's perhaps most disappointing that the United States—a nation founded on Christian principles—is losing its Christian base at an alarming rate.

How can these things be? Our country is saturated with Christian bookstores, radio stations, television programs, and schools. And yet for all of this Christian influence, it seems that the United States is rapidly becoming a pagan nation. It's tempting to think that we should be fighting social issues and not wasting time on "academic" topics like origins.

But what if there were a connection between origins and all these social issues? I suggest that there is, in fact, a very strong connection. The social issues many Christians find distressing are not problems in themselves, but rather, they are symptoms of an underlying root cause—the loss of biblical authority stemming from attacks on the book of Genesis. Christian values cannot exist in isolation; they only make sense in light of the history recorded in Genesis. So, as society increasingly rejects Genesis in favor of evolution or an old-earth creation view, it is a natural

> ❖
>
> *Christian values cannot exist in isolation; they only make sense in light of the history recorded in Genesis.*
>
> ❖

consequence that we will experience the decline of Christian America.

Where do Christian doctrines such as "marriage" originate? This doctrine goes back to Genesis. God instituted the family unit. He created Adam and then Eve from Adam's side, and this was the first married couple. Genesis 2:24 tells us that this historical event is the reason for marriage. The Bible defines marriage as one man and one woman united in God for life. Jesus affirmed this in Matthew 19:4-6, and He quoted Genesis to prove His point.

But if the history in Genesis were not true, then why would marriage have to be so defined? Why not a man and a man, or a man and a rock, for that matter? Without the foundational history in Genesis, marriage is simply reduced to a cultural trend—one that is subject to the shifting winds of human opinions and feelings. It's not surprising that marriage is under attack today, since its foundation in Genesis is being undermined by evolutionary dogma.

Likewise, the sanctity of human life, human freedom, laws, and justice—all of these have their foundation in the literal, historical understanding of Genesis. And yet, Genesis continues to be attacked throughout our culture. We are told that millions of years of evolution resulted in all life on earth. And as more people reject biblical history, the more we will see the decay of Christianity. Individuals may believe in evolution and still behave in a Christian fashion, but their belief and behavior remain logically inconsistent. People will tend to act on what they believe. And the more people believe in evolution, the more they will behave as those who reject God as Creator.

If we are ever going to see America turn back to God, we must faithfully teach and defend the Bible—starting with the creation account in Genesis.

CHRISTIAN DOCTRINE AND GENESIS

I s the decline of Christianity in society really connected to the rejection of the historical understanding of Genesis? Christian doctrines are found throughout the Bible. So it is tempting to think that we could reject Genesis without affecting the rest of Scripture. But this would be a mistake. Every major Christian doctrine is rooted in the book of Genesis. And while these doctrines are mentioned elsewhere in the Bible, they cannot stand up to scrutiny apart from a literal Genesis any more than a tree can survive without its roots or a house can stand with no foundation. Let's consider some Christian doctrines and see how they are established in Genesis.

> *Every major Christian doctrine is rooted in the book of Genesis.*

1. Marriage. The Bible teaches that marriage is a sacred union between one man and one woman for life. There are any number of passages in Scripture that address the topic of marriage. But where does the idea of marriage originate? God instituted marriage on the sixth day of creation. He made Eve from Adam's side to be a helper to her husband. The Bible specifically tells us in Genesis 2:24 that this historical event is the reason why we have marriage today. "Therefore a man shall leave his father and mother and be joined to his wife, and they shall become one flesh." There can be no doubt that this is the foundation of marriage because the Bible specifically tells us as much. Marriage is one man and one woman united by God for life because that's the way God established it at creation. God provided the prototype marriage, and we are commanded to follow His example. Jesus affirmed this in Matthew 19:4-6.

Can the doctrine of marriage be defended apart from its foundation in Genesis? If Genesis were not true, could we still argue that marriage must be defined as a union between one man and one woman for life? Some have argued for traditional marriage simply because it is tradition. But traditions don't obligate others to the same behavior; just because you hide Easter eggs doesn't mean that others must do so. Some people wear costumes on Halloween, but that doesn't mean that you should. Likewise, just because marriage has traditionally been one way in our culture doesn't logically imply that it must continue to be that way. Cultures change, and so do traditions.

If Genesis were not true, could we still argue that marriage must be defined as a union between one man and one woman for life?

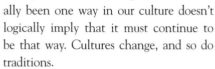

Some people have argued for traditional marriage because it just seems right to them. But then, of course, others will argue that a homosexual union seems right. Subjective feelings don't provide a logical foundation for anything. Some might argue that marriage should be one man and one woman for life because that is what the majority believes. But a majority opinion doesn't make something right. Again, if a majority of people dress up on Halloween, does that mean that you should? If a majority of people like pickles on their hamburgers does that make it morally wrong for you to not like pickles on your hamburger? Clearly not.

If evolution were true, then there would be no fundamental basis for the doctrine of marriage. Marriage would simply be a cultural trend—one that is now evolving into something quite different than it was years ago.

But the fact remains that marriage is defined as the union between one man and one woman for life because the Creator established it this way from the beginning and recorded this event for us in the book of Genesis. Additionally, the vital passages about marriage elsewhere in Scripture all harken back to Genesis and the creation account. Genesis—the historical record of God's work in creation—is the basis for the doctrine of marriage.

2. Sanctity of Human Life. The Bible teaches that human beings are qualitatively different from other biological organisms. We are made in the image of God and enjoy special rights that animals and plants do not. This is why it is fundamentally immoral to murder a human being; we dare not mar the image of God in such a way. And yet most people give little thought to the life that was extinguished in order for them to enjoy a good hamburger or fish sandwich. For that matter, every time we take a breath of air, multitudes of microorganisms are absorbed into our body and destroyed by our immune system.[1] Why is it that no one cries "murder" when we consume a turnip? The reason is this: Everyone knows in his heart-of-hearts that plants and animals do not bear the image of God, but people do. Whether we admit it or not, we all recognize that human beings are not just another organism on the planet. We are set apart from animals and plants by the Creator Himself, having been made in His image.

❖

We are made in the image of God and enjoy special rights that animals and plants do not.

❖

And where do you suppose this biblical principle originates? In Genesis.

> So God created man in His own image; in the image of God He created him; male and female He created them. And God blessed them, and God said to them, "Be fruitful and multiply; fill the earth and subdue it; have dominion over the fish of the sea, over the birds of the air, and over every living thing that moves on the earth." (Genesis 1:27-28)

Plants were made for people to eat (Genesis 1:29). "Killing" a carrot and consuming it presents no moral dilemma—God created it for that purpose. In Genesis 9:2-3, God extends our diet to include animals as well. But the murder of a human being is unacceptable (Genesis 4:8-12; 9:6). The sanctity of human life is an ethical truth with its foundation in Genesis.

But if creation were just a myth, if people were simply evolved animals, then how could they be distinct from animals? Animals have no moral code. If a lion kills another lion, we don't say that it is "wrong," and we don't put the lion in jail. What one animal does to another is morally irrelevant. So how could the act of murder be considered wrong if humans were no different than animals? Any distinction would be arbitrary and subjective.

Someone might argue that humans are more intelligent than "other" animals, which is why humans have more rights and should not be killed. But this standard is arbitrary and leads to the bizarre conclusion that smart humans have more rights than less intelligent ones. Should a person with a very high I.Q. be allowed to kill someone with a very low I.Q.? Clearly not, and yet that is the inevitable conclusion of such thinking. From an evolutionary perspective, human beings are not fundamentally different from animals or plants. Consequently, any line of evolutionary thinking that justifies killing animals or plants can also be applied to a particular group of people based on subjective criteria such as ethnicity, age, ability, or gender.

Why not abort inconvenient babies if they are just distant cousins of broccoli (as evolutionists believe)? Many have used this type of argument for abortion, but such reasoning doesn't end with the unborn. Why not dispose of an inconvenient child shortly after birth? Why not kill an ungrateful teenager, or the elderly and infirm? Clearly, most evolutionists would join us in adamantly denouncing such actions. But the point is that they cannot account for *why such atrocities would be wrong* from an evolutionary perspective. They may not emotionally like such things. But they cannot provide a logical reason to call such actions wrong.

Only the Christian worldview can provide a logical foundation for denouncing murder as fundamentally *wrong*. Evolution is not logically consistent with the sanctity of human life. But the Bible is. God has defined life and distinguished human life from any other form of life—and He established these facts in the book of Genesis.

3. Clothing. While it's not a doctrine we hear preached in many sermons, clothing is a Christian doctrine that can be traced back to Genesis. Clothing was originally unnecessary, but it was introduced as a covering for Adam and Eve because of the shame associated with their sin (Genesis 2:25; 3:1-7; 3:21). This is why virtually all cultures in the world have some form of modesty when it comes to clothing, even in the hottest climates on earth.

But how do we make sense of clothing apart from the historical account in Genesis?

But how do we make sense of clothing apart from the historical account in Genesis? From an evolutionary perspective, in which people are not fundamentally different from any other organism, why wear clothes when it is warm outside? After all, animals don't wear clothes.[2] And if humans are simply evolved animals, then why should it matter?

And yet, the need for clothing is intuitive for all of us. Shame is innately associated with nakedness. We all feel embarrassment. In fact, most societies have laws regulating public modesty. But animals aren't embarrassed by their lack of clothing. Shame has no place in evolution, but even an evolutionist would be embarrassed to be caught naked in public.

We cover ourselves because God established the necessity for clothing, not for the sake of enhancing beauty, but rather to relieve the shame and embarrassment caused by original sin, which was described so carefully in Genesis after the Fall of mankind. Without a historical Genesis, the foundational doctrines of life and faith have no basis.

4. Laws. Not only are we a nation of laws, but we are also people with innate understanding of and respect for laws. All laws—civil and moral—have one thing in common: they put limitations on our behavior by threatening some sort of penalty if we do not comply. The Bible has recorded a number of laws that guide and constrain our actions, whether as a nation or as individuals. But where did the first laws originate? And why should we have laws anyway?

> ❖
>
> *But where did the first laws originate? And why should we have laws anyway?*
>
> ❖

To discover the origin of laws, we look to Genesis. The first laws were given to human beings by God—He told Adam and Eve to go and multiply and rule over the creatures of the earth (Genesis 1:28). God also told Adam not to eat from the tree of the knowledge of good and evil, and He attached a penalty for disobedience—death.

We have laws because our Creator God made man in His image—to be a special creation with a unique relationship with Him. He has the right to set rules for our behavior. And since God gave us freedom of choice—we are not mindless robots—there are both consequences for disobedience and blessings for obedience (e.g., Deuteronomy 28:1-14). We owe God our very existence, and so we have a moral obligation to obey any laws He has set forth. But we also know that He will hold us accountable for our actions. We often experience consequences in this world, but they aren't always immediately evident. However, we will all face a final judgment. When naturally rebellious humans create societies, civil laws are necessary to restrain evil in society. Laws make sense in light of Genesis.

But from an evolutionary perspective, in which humans are just animals, are laws reasonable? Animals do not have laws. They do what they want without any sense of fairness or justice. They have no government, no police, no crimes, and no penalties. Animals do what animals do; we don't put a lion in jail if it kills another lion. So why do we put a human in jail if he kills another human?

The idea of evolution requires the concept of "survival of the fittest." The strong dominate the weak in a competition for resources, which eventually eliminates the weak, leading to a stronger, more adapted organism. Humans allegedly evolved from less fit organisms in this manner. But if this were true, then how could we make sense of laws? Evolution is all about the strong overcoming the weak; so why have any laws to protect the weak from the strong? Laws fundamentally prevent the stronger, the more "fit" person, from killing or otherwise abusing the weaker person. Laws run counter to the notion of survival of the fittest. Most evolutionists believe in laws, but such beliefs don't make sense if evolution were really true.

5. Seven-Day Week. The Fourth Commandment states: "Remember the Sabbath day, to keep it holy" (Exodus 20:8). God's instruction is for us to take one day a week to rest and honor Him. Most Christians celebrate the Sabbath on Sunday, to honor the resurrection of Christ. But even non-Christians usually take at least one day in seven to rest. In fact, most cultures on earth have a seven-day week. But where does this idea come from? And why rest one day in *seven*, as opposed to ten or five? Where does our seven-day week come from? While the Fourth Commandment is first listed in Exodus 20:8, the idea originates in Genesis.

> *There is no secular basis for a seven-day week. All other units of time have a foundation in astronomy.*

Genesis 1:1-2:2 indicates that God created in six days and then rested one day. Of course, the all-powerful God does not need to rest. Nor did He really require six days to make the universe—He had the power to do it all instantaneously. God created in six days and then rested one day as a pattern for us. Exodus 20:11 explains that our work week is based on the creation week.

> For in six days the LORD made the heavens and the earth, the sea, and all that is in them, and rested the seventh day. Therefore the LORD blessed the Sabbath day and hallowed it. (Exodus 20:11)

There is no secular basis for a seven-day week. All other units of time have a foundation in astronomy: a day is the amount of time for earth to rotate once with respect to the sun, a month is the amount of time for the moon to go through all its phases, and a year is the amount of time it takes the earth to orbit the sun. But there is no common astronomical phenomenon that corresponds to one week. Some have speculated that our ancient ancestors invented the week in honor of the five planets that are visible without a telescope (besides earth), the sun, and the moon. But there is no time function here. Why seven *days*, and not years or hours, or pounds or inches? The number of planets has nothing to do with time, so it doesn't make sense as a starting point for determining the number of days in a week. It is far more reasonable to suppose that days of the week were *later* named in association with the planets, the sun, and the moon since they are both seven in number. As far as we know, the only basis for our seven-day week comes from the pattern established in Genesis. And so the fact that most cultures on earth have a seven-day week is evidence that they all had prior knowledge about Genesis.

6. The Gospel. Most Christians realize that the central most important doctrine of Christianity is the gospel—the good news that Jesus died on the cross to pay for our sins. But where do ideas like "sin" come from? When did we learn that death was the penalty for sin? At what point did mankind understand that he needed a Savior? All of the concepts necessary to comprehend the gospel have their foundation in Genesis.

Romans 6:23 tells us that the wages of sin is death. But the connection between sin and death does not originate in the book of Romans; it originates in Genesis. Genesis teaches us that God is our Creator and that we are made in His image (Genesis 1:26-27). As such, we owe Him our lives and our obedience. Genesis teaches us that God holds people accountable for

> *Their perfect fellowship with God was broken by their treason; they would now age and eventually die for their insidious crime against their loving Creator.*

their actions—there is a penalty associated with disobedience to God (Genesis 2:17). Therefore, we have motivation to obey God.

In Genesis, we learn that the world was once absolutely perfect, the "very good" creation of an infinitely holy and loving God. He instructed Adam to rule over this world as a good steward, serving under the authority of his Creator and having authority over every other creature. If Adam obeyed God, he would live forever in perfect fellowship with God, enjoying the perfection of the world. But God is righteous and will not tolerate evil. After God created Adam, He told him not to eat from the tree of the knowledge of good and evil (Genesis 2:17). If Adam disobeyed, then there would be punishment—he would immediately become mortal and eventually die (Genesis 2:17; 3:17-19).

Nothing in the text of Scripture indicates that the tree had some kind of mystical properties. It is simply what God chose as a test of Adam's allegiance. Adam could choose to submit to God as his Lord, learning from Him and interpreting experience in light of God's revealed knowledge. Or he could choose to be a "god" unto himself, rejecting the commandment of the Lord, interpreting all experience in terms of his own arbitrary rules and limited thinking. Sadly, Adam chose the latter, having been tempted by his wife Eve, who had been tempted by the serpent. And in that moment, Adam and Eve became mortal beings. Their perfect fellowship with God was broken by their treason; they would now age and eventually die for their insidious crime against their loving Creator.

❖

One day, a perfect "Lamb"—a descendant of Eve and yet also God Himself—would die so that Adam and Eve could live again, forever in perfection with their Creator.

❖

The entire world was marred by Adam's sin. Animals now suffer pain and death (Romans 8:20-22; Genesis 1:31), just like Adam. Why? Adam was in charge of the world, and so his sin affected everything and everyone under his authority, in somewhat the same manner in which people today suffer when their leaders make foolish decisions—when the President of the United States makes a bad decision, it has a negative effect on all people throughout the country because those individuals are under the President's authority. It may seem unfair that animals suffer and die as a result of Adam's actions. However, if the world remained perfect and unchanged after sin was introduced in the garden, then that would indicate that God had not really given Adam authority over it as He had pronounced at creation—an unchanged garden would signal that God had lied. But God does not lie (Hebrews 6:18). The integrity of God demands that both Adam and the world suffer a curse as the right penalty for Adam's sin.

As descendants of Adam and Eve, we have inherited a sin nature—we are conceived in a state that is alienated from God's perfect glory, a condition that rebels against God. But God was merciful to humanity. Rather than leaving Adam and Eve to die eternally for their rebellion, God promised that He would provide a Savior, someone to pay the penalty of death for Adam and Eve so they could eventually be restored into perfect fellowship with God. God told them that the "seed of the woman"—a descendant of Eve—would accomplish this. As a symbol of that coming salvation, God killed an animal or animals (perhaps a lamb) to provide clothing for Adam and Eve. These skins covered the shame of their treason and showed them the nature of their salvation. One day, a perfect "Lamb"—a descendant of Eve and yet also God Himself—would die so that Adam and Eve could live again, forever in perfection with their Creator. The gospel message is rooted in Genesis!

But apart from Genesis, the gospel message makes no sense. Death has always existed in the evolutionary worldview—long before people. So how could death be the penalty for sin? And if death is not the penalty for sin, then why did Jesus die on a cross? Is the concept of "sin" even meaningful in an evolutionary universe? If the world has always been full of suffering and death, then why would anyone think that he needs to be reconciled with God?

The Bible teaches that we may only be redeemed (freed from the slavery of sin) by a blood relative (Leviticus 25:47-49). There are a number of reasons for this requirement, but we won't address them in this book. The point is that only a human being—a blood relative—can be our savior. God became a man to save us as our "kinsman-redeemer." Jesus is not only God, but He is also our blood relative. Thus, His shed blood counts as ours. The Bible makes it very clear that the blood of animals cannot pay for sin (Hebrews 10:4). The reason: We are not related to animals. But if evolution were true, then animals could also be our savior, since we would be related to them. If we evolved from animals, then there would have been no need for Jesus to die on the cross.

We certainly do *not* mean that a person who believes in evolution cannot be a Christian. Clearly, someone can be a genuine Christian, having professed Christ as Lord and serving him faithfully in many ways, and yet still believe in a theistic form of evolution. But those two beliefs (Christianity and evolution) would be inconsistent with each other. Like water and oil, evolution and Christianity simply do not mix. Fortunately, logical consistency in our beliefs is not a requirement for salvation, or we would all be in trouble! God shows mercy on us, even when our thinking is muddled. But that doesn't mean that we should continue living with muddled thinking. Honoring God's Word as our supreme and ultimate standard, consistent biblical reasoning, and dependence on the truths found in Scripture exhibit gratitude for the salvation He provided. All Christian doctrines only make sense in light of the history of Genesis.

Morality without History?

In response to all of the above, some Christians might say, "Yes, Christian doctrines do go back to the stories in Genesis. But that doesn't mean it has to be real history. The Bible is a morality book, not a history book. It's a bit like the tortoise and the hare," they say. "You get the point of the story, even though no one believes that it really happened."

But this is a false analogy. Genesis is written as history. It gives the historical basis for holding to Christian doctrines. That's quite different from a fable like the tortoise and the hare. A fable does not provide a *foundation* for morality; it merely illustrates a truth (perhaps a moral truth) that people already know. If someone doesn't understand a moral truth, a fable can clarify how to apply it. But if someone does not believe in a moral claim, a fictional story about its application would be irrelevant! A fable can illustrate a truth, but it cannot provide the *foundation* for a truth, since it is not itself true. *Truth cannot be based in fiction!* The moral principles established in Genesis can only be true if the history in Genesis is literally true.

> *A fable can illustrate a truth, but it cannot provide the foundation for a truth, since it is not itself true. Truth cannot be based in fiction!*

COMMONSENSE BIBLE INTERPRETATION

Since our culture is so saturated with evolutionary teaching, it can be a strong temptation for Christians to attempt to merge evolutionary ideas with biblical truth. Is this possible? After all, Christians sometimes disagree about the interpretation of difficult verses. So why can't Genesis be interpreted as being consistent with evolution?

Approaching Genesis in a commonsense fashion—reading it in a straightforward manner—will nowhere evoke any concept of mutation and "natural selection" acting over millions of years. It clearly speaks of a Creator who supernaturally spoke into existence discrete kinds of plants and animals, along with a unique creature called "man," within six 24-hour days. Of course, you can interpret Genesis, and any other part of the Bible, any way that you like—as if it were poetry, metaphors, or symbolism. Or you could just take it at face value. (You could also do that with a science textbook!)

So, while there could be multiple interpretations of Scripture, not all interpretations would be correct. The authors of the Bible (or any other book) had a particular meaning in mind when they penned the text. The *correct* interpretation is that which corresponds to the author's intention.

> *The authors of the Bible (or any other book) had a particular meaning in mind when they penned the text.*

And God, as the Author of a unified and perfectly inspired book we call the Bible, is to be acknowledged as being the Author of truth—not error or confusion.

Exegesis is the act of understanding the author's intention: pulling out of a text the meaning that the author placed into it. Eisegesis is the opposite; it is the act of reading into a text what the author did not intend. When we read the

Bible, we must seek to understand what the Lord (through the various human writers) intended when He first revealed His Word to them. And that common-sense approach begins where God began His revelation—in Genesis 1:1.

Literary Genres in Scripture

Context is crucial when we study Bible passages. We need to ask, "What type of literature are we reading?" Poetry? History? Prophecy? The Bible contains several different types of literature. Fortunately, it is usually easy to recognize from context the type of literature under investigation.

Poetry

The Psalms are wonderful examples of poetic writing in the Bible, many of which are songs that would have been sung by the readers; context makes this clear. When we consider the preamble for Psalm 19:1—"To the Chief Musician. A Psalm of David"—can there be any doubt that it expresses the lyrics for an ancient song of praise?

We often think of poetry in terms of rhyme and meter, but the ancient Hebrews crafted their poetic writings using "parallelism." Parallelism involves a twofold (or more) structure in which a statement is made and then followed up by something logically connected to it. There are two types of parallelism. The first is called "synonymous parallelism," in which a statement is followed by another statement with basically the same meaning, while using different words. The second statement often contains synonyms of the words used in the first statement.

> *We often think of poetry in terms of rhyme and meter, but the ancient Hebrews crafted their poetic writings using "parallelism."*

Psalm 19:1 is a great example: "The heavens declare the glory of God; And the firmament shows His handiwork." The second part of the verse is basically a restatement of the first part, but using different words. "Firmament" is a synonym for "heavens," and "the glory of God" is shown through "His handiwork." Psalm 19:2 continues this parallelism: "Day unto day utters speech, And night unto night reveals knowledge." "Day unto day" basically means "continually," and so does "night unto night." Likewise, uttering speech and revealing knowledge are tightly connected.

The other type of parallelism is called "antithetical parallelism," in which a statement is followed by a *contrasting* principle. For example, in Proverbs 1:7 we read, "The fear of the LORD is the beginning of knowledge, But fools despise wisdom and instruction." The first part of the verse contrasts the wise person, who has respect for the Lord, with the fool, who hates wisdom and instruction.

Parallelism is key to recognizing poetic language in the Bible. As with modern poetry, poetic language is not intended to be taken in a wooden literal sense. It frequently uses figures of speech to convey the author's intention. Thus, Isaiah 55:12 should not be read as a literal indication that trees would somehow grow hands and then clap them; we understand the figure of speech as a portrayal of nature "rejoicing" at the coming of the Lord.

Can Genesis be interpreted as poetic? Does it bear the marks of either synonymous or antithetical parallelism? Not at all.

We find no trace of parallelism in the events recorded in Genesis 1. Occasionally, someone suggests that the phrase "so the evening and the morning" represents poetry. While this phrase is repeated at the close of each day of creation, it is *not* synonymous parallelism. Remember, synonymous parallelism involves stating basically the same thing using *different* words. But the wording here is identical. No synonyms are used at all. Moreover, parallelism usually involves the very next statement. But the close of each creation day is separated by the events that happened on each day. There really is no legitimate evidence of parallelism or any other poetic device in Genesis 1. Moses did not intend it to be taken as poetry—if we want to understand the meaning, we must not approach Genesis as a book of poetry.

Parables

Jesus often spoke in parables, short stories that clarify spiritual or moral truths. Jesus tells parables of the landowner (Matthew 21:33-40), the Good Samaritan (Luke 10:30-36), the seed (Luke 8:4-8), and others. Parables need not be literally true; instead, we are supposed to consider them as illustrations of moral or spiritual principles. We can eas-

Genesis 1 does not involve common, everyday experiences—nothing could be less common to our experience than God speaking the universe into existence!

ily recognize parables by certain contextual clues.

1. Parables rarely give specific names or irrelevant details. Instead, they keep facts very generic: "A certain man" (Luke 10:30).

2. Parables involve common, everyday experience. We are all familiar with planting a seed and how it is affected by various types of soil. So, the parable of the seed assumes that the listener understands the common knowledge associated with soil conditions.

3. Parables illustrate moral or spiritual principles from common experiences. In the case of the seed, the principle is clear—different people in different circumstances will have different responses when presented with the gospel message (Luke 8:11-15).

Could Genesis be a parable? Some have tried to interpret it that way. But Genesis does not bear any of the contextual marks of a parable.

1. Genesis lacks the generality of a parable. Instead, it gives specific names (Adam and Eve, Cain and Abel) and specific details (the location of Eden, the description of the rivers, etc.) (Genesis 2:5-15). In fact, Genesis 5 gives a detailed genealogy beginning with Adam and listing the specific names and ages of his descendants through Noah. No parable has such detailed chronology.

2. Genesis 1 does not involve common, everyday experiences—nothing could be less common to our experience than God speaking the universe into existence!

3. Genesis is not written as an illustration of a moral teaching through a common experience. The historical accounts in Genesis do provide the basis for morality, but Genesis is about as opposite to a parable as anything could be.

History

The Bible also contains historical narrative, one of the most common types of literature found in Scripture. Historical narrative is the straight-forward record of events that have actually happened, usually from the perspective of an eyewitness, such as the book of Acts or the gospels. The book of Exodus is primarily historical in nature. It records the history of the Israelites' rescue from their captivity in Egypt.

Historical narrative is to be taken in a literal sense, with allowances for occasional obvious figures of speech. After all, when we read that George Washington was the first President of the United States, we don't scratch our heads trying to interpret the symbolic meaning. Clearly, it means what it states. Historical narrative is marked by the listing of specific names, dates, and details that may or may not be essential to the narrative.

In Hebrew writing, historical narrative is also distinguished by what is called the "*vav* consecutive." *Vav* or *waw* is the Hebrew word (and letter) usually translated "and" in English Bibles. When a sentence starts with "and" that is followed by a verb (in the Hebrew word order and of the right form), it is a *vav* consecutive and indicates historical narrative, as in a chain of events.

For example, Genesis 1:6—"And God said"—in Hebrew is worded "and said God." This is the *vav* consecutive. Almost all the verses in Genesis 1 are *vav* consecutive, which is why many translations of Genesis 1 (such as the King James Version used in this example) begin almost every verse with the word "and." It may sound awkward in English (and some translations omit some of the "ands" for that very reason), but the structure is indicative of Hebrew historical narrative. Basically, Genesis 1 is telling us, "This happened, and then this happened, and then this happened, and then...."

Good evidence suggests that Moses got much of his information from previous documents that had been written by eyewitnesses.

Genesis also gives specific names (as in the genealogies in Genesis 5) and other specific details about real events. Although Genesis was written by Moses under the guidance of the Holy Spirit, good evidence suggests that Moses got much of his information from previous documents that had been written by eyewitnesses. This is implied by the phrase "these are the generations of." The word "generations" can literally be translated as "origin" or "history." This phrase appears to be naming the author of the corresponding section.

The evidence is clear; Genesis is a book of history. It does not contain the marks of poetry or parables. Instead, it contains all the marks of ordinary historical narrative. From context, there can be no doubt that Moses intended

Genesis to be taken as the literal history of the first ~2,000 years of the universe. If readers choose *not* to take it that way, then their interpretation will not match the meaning of the text. In other words, their interpretation will simply be wrong.

Letting Scripture Interpret Scripture

Not only can we learn from grammar and context, but the Bible itself teaches us how we should approach Scripture. Studying the manner in which the authors of Scripture interpreted other passages in the Bible provides examples of how to conduct good Bible interpretation. This is no more obvious than with the Author of all Scripture—the Lord Jesus Himself. So how did Jesus interpret Genesis?

Jesus and Genesis

Jesus often quoted the Old Testament Scriptures. He responded to critics with "It is written" and "Have you not read," followed by a relevant scriptural quotation (e.g., Matthew 4:4; 12:3). But it sometimes surprises people to learn how often Jesus quoted from the book of Genesis—the number of references to Genesis is as high as all the other Old Testament references *combined*. Roughly half of Christ's references to Scripture were quotations from Genesis. He obviously understood the importance of origins.

> *There is no hint that Jesus took any of the narrative of Genesis as anything less than literal history.*

Moreover, Jesus did not take Genesis as a metaphor, poetry, a parable, or a myth. He took it as literal history. When Jesus spoke of Moses, He referred to him as a real historical person (John 5:46-47). There is no hint that Jesus took any of the narrative of Genesis as anything less than literal history. In fact, Christ understood that the moral truths of Christianity have their foundation in the historical accounts of Genesis. This is demonstrated with the doctrine of marriage.

In Matthew 19:3-12, the critics of Christ asked Him about divorce. Specifically, they wanted to know if a man could divorce his wife for any reason. Christ explained that divorce was only permitted for cases of infidelity. He went on to explain that laws about divorce were made necessary because of the sinful hardheartedness of man. That is, if human beings were righteous in all their attitudes and actions, then divorce laws would be totally unnecessary because there would be no such thing as infidelity. Had human beings not fallen into sin, then divorce would be unnecessary. God intended marriage to be one man and one woman united for life. Thus, Jesus quotes Genesis 1 and 2. Christ understood that the basis for the doctrine of marriage (as well as the unfortunate need for laws concerning divorce) is found in a historical Genesis.

Some people have erroneously claimed that Genesis 1 and 2 are two different and contradictory creation accounts. However, Jesus (the One who inspired the text of Genesis) quoted them in the same breath. He saw no contradiction because there isn't one. Genesis 2 is simply a more detailed description of the events of the sixth day of creation.

Many Christians are tempted to try to blend a belief in evolution with their faith in Christ. But Christ clearly accepted a literal Genesis. Why shouldn't every follower of Christ? If we cannot trust that Jesus was right about the history of the world, then how can we trust anything else He taught?

The Apostles and Genesis

The apostles also understood Genesis to be literal history. Paul, who wrote nearly half of the books of the New Testament, referred to Adam and Eve as historical people (see Romans 5:12-14; 1 Corinthians 15:21-22; 2 Corinthians 11:3) and based Christian doctrine on this fact (e.g., 1 Timothy 2:12-15). Indeed, the entire theological system espoused by Paul would come crashing down if Genesis were not literal history. For example, Paul contrasts Adam with Christ in 1 Corinthians 15:21-22. He refers to Christ as the "last Adam" who takes Adam's place on the cross (1 Corinthians 15:45-47). If Adam were just a fictional character, then Paul's comparison would make no sense.

The apostle Peter also took Genesis literally. He wrote about Noah and the Flood as real history (1 Peter 3:20; 2 Peter 2:5). The apostle John clearly believed Genesis was real history, since he wrote about Cain and Abel (1 John 3:12). Jude also referred to people, places, and events in Genesis: Sodom and Gomorrah (Jude 7), Moses (Jude

❖

Indeed, the entire theological system espoused by Paul would come crashing down if Genesis were not literal history.

❖

9), and Cain (Jude 11). James referred to Abraham as a real person (James 2:21). The author of Hebrews referred to a number of people in Genesis as real historical figures: Cain and Abel (Hebrews 11:4), Enoch (Hebrews 11:5), Noah (Hebrews 11:7), and Abraham (Hebrews 11:8). The author's argument in Hebrews 11 would make no sense if these were fictional characters. Nowhere does the Bible ever suggest that Genesis should be taken as anything other than real, literal history.

3

THE TIMESCALE OF CREATION

Genesis cannot be exegetically read in a way that is compatible with evolution. Moses intended us to understand that God created the heavens and earth supernaturally. God spoke into existence things that had no previous existence. But how long did the work of creation take, and how long ago did God create the universe?

A straightforward reading of Genesis suggests the following:

1. God created heaven, earth, and everything within them in the span of six days and then rested on the seventh day.

2. The creation week occurred roughly 6,000 years ago, determined from calculations in the genealogies and acknowledging that Abraham lived around 2,000 B.C.

3. The Flood described in Genesis 6-8 was worldwide, destroying all land animals and people except those preserved on Noah's Ark. Although the Bible does not specifically say so, it seems a reasonable inference that most of the fossils we find on earth today resulted from that Flood.

But how long did the work of creation take, and how long ago did God create the universe?

Thus, if Genesis is, as we have shown, accurate historical narrative, then it is also natural to conclude that the author of Genesis really did intend to convey the idea that creation took place in six days, a few thousand years ago, and that Noah's Flood was a real event, worldwide in extent.

This, of course, runs contrary to what people are taught in most schools. We are normally taught that the earth is 4.5 billion years old and that the universe is even older—approximately 13 billion years old! The process of earth's forming supposedly took millions of years, not six days. The fossils were allegedly deposited over hundreds of millions of years, not by a catastrophic flood. In fact, the conventional secular opinion is that earth has never been completely covered by water. We are told that radiometric dating proves that earth is indeed billions of years old. So, it is very tempting for Christians to bend the text of Genesis to accommodate the secular timescale. But given that Genesis is historical narrative, the text must be read in a straightforward manner if we are to be true to the author's intention. So how could anyone argue that Genesis allows for vast ages?

Some people would (correctly) point out that even historical narrative contains occasional figures of speech. They might also (correctly) point out that words are not always translated properly from the original Hebrew language into English. Is it possible, therefore, that Genesis allows for vast lengths of time? Could we be misunderstanding the text due to a mistranslation or an unfamiliar figure of speech?

The Day-Age Position

Some have argued that the word translated as "day" in Genesis 1 should really be translated "age." Hence, they claim that God did not create in six ordinary, literal days, but rather over six long ages of time—each millions of years in length. They may state that Genesis is historical, but that it has been mis-

Is this passage really addressing the days of creation and telling us that they are actually thousands of years each? Not at all.

translated and therefore misunderstood. Unfortunately, this "day-age" position has become quite popular in the church. Proponents point out that the Hebrew word *yom*, which is translated as "day" in Genesis 1, occasionally means a period of time longer than 24 hours, e.g., "in the days of Saul" (1 Chronicles 5:10) or "the day of the LORD" (Joel 2:1).

It is certainly true that *yom* can mean a period of time longer than 24 hours in certain contexts, but does it mean "age" in Genesis? Day-Age advocates often attempt to provide support for their position by citing a portion of 2 Peter 3:8, "with the Lord one day is as a thousand years." They claim this verse means that time is very different to God, and so the days of Genesis should not be understood as ordinary days from a human perspective, but they should be considered as long periods of time. Is this passage really addressing the days of creation and telling us that they are actually thousands of years each? Not at all. The context is actually dealing with the apparent delay in God's promise to come again; it is not referring to the days of creation at all!

Even if Peter was indicating that the days of creation were a thousand years each, this would not help the Day-Age advocate because it would mean the earth is about 12,000 years old instead of 6,000. Proponents of the Day-Age position attempt to line up the Bible's teaching with the secular timescale of *billions* of years.

It is also noteworthy that Day-Age advocates usually only quote the first part of the verse. They leave out the last part. While the passage says that a day is as a thousand years with God, it continues with "a thousand years as one day." If it is reasonable to use the first part of the verse to make time longer, then logically it must be reasonable to use the second part to make time shorter. We could then argue that the 2,000 years between Adam and Abraham was really only two 24-hour days since "a thousand years [is] as one day." How absurd! And yet those who seek to compromise the accuracy of Genesis don't see the absurdity of applying this same line of thinking to the first part of the verse.

2 Peter 3:8 is simply indicating that God is beyond time—it doesn't bother God to wait a thousand years any more than it does to wait one day. Some might still try to alter the timescale in Genesis by saying, "Since God is beyond time, when He talks about 'days' it could mean any period of time." But this isn't logical. Since God is indeed beyond time, we must presume that when God does use words referring to lengths of time, they are to be understood from a human perspective.

"Day" in Context

The Hebrew word for "day" (*yom*) can actually mean one of several things depending on context. Perhaps not surprisingly, its ordinary meaning is a 24-hour day or the light portion thereof. It can also mean a year, as well as an unspecified period of time. But that is also true of our English word for "day." You have probably heard expressions like "back in the day" in which "day" is used figuratively as an unspecified period of time. The word can even be used in two or more ways within the same sentence: "In my grandfather's day, it took four days to drive across Texas." There is no doubt that the first occurrence means "time" in a generic sense, and the second occurrence means an ordinary 24-hour day since it is preceded by a number. The context determines the meaning.

It's the same with the Hebrew word for "day"—the context makes the meaning clear. For example, in Hebrew, when "day" is used with a number as part of an ordered list ("the first day, the second day, the third day"), it is always translated as "day" (there are no exceptions in the Bible) and always clearly means an ordinary day. When Jonah was in the great fish for "three days," there can be no doubt that these are 24-hour days, not years or unspecified units of time.

When "day" is mentioned in the context of "morning," it clearly means an ordinary day. For example, "morning seemed to come early that day." Likewise, when mentioned in the context of "evening," it is obviously referring to an ordinary day. Such expressions occur 23 times each in the Old Testament (not including Genesis 1), and there is really no disagreement that those other passages are referring to ordinary days. When "evening" and "morning" are combined, this obviously refers to an ordinary day, even if the word "day" is not used, since evening and morning mark the boundaries of the day. When the word "day" is contrasted with "night," it is clearly an ordinary day. This contrast occurs over 50 times outside of Genesis 1, and no one doubts that these refer to ordinary days.

What do we learn from the context of Genesis 1? Consider verse five, "God called the light Day, and the darkness He called Night. So the evening and the morning were the first day." In the first sentence we find the word "day" contrasted with "night." This indicates an ordinary day. In the second sentence we see "day" associated with a number, as in "one day" (or some translations read "the first day"). This indicates an ordinary day. We also see the word "day" contextually associated with "morning" and "evening"—each of which constrains the meaning of *yom* to that of an ordinary day, not some unspecified period of time. Furthermore, the occurrence of "evening" and "morning" together constitutes an ordinary day. Considering the context,

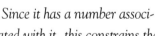

Since it has a number associated with it, this constrains the meaning to an ordinary day.

a literal interpretation of this passage makes the meaning very clear—the first day of creation is an ordinary 24-hour day!

What about the other days of creation? Each of these verses contain sentences structured with the phrase, "So the evening and the morning were the [first, second, third, etc.] day." Each of the six days of creation contains at least *four* contextual markers, any one of which constrains the meaning of "day" to that of an ordinary day. It appears that God did not want there to be any possible misunderstanding of the length of the days. Thus, we can be certain that the creation week consisted of six days in the literal, ordinary sense of the word.

What about the seventh day? The biblical text does not associate the seventh day with the words "evening" and "morning." Some have suggested that this might allow them to fit the billions of years into the seventh day. But such thinking is erroneous.

First of all, the seventh day of creation appears in context with a number. Genesis 2:2-3 refers to the seventh day as the day when God rested. Since it has a number associated with it, this constrains the meaning to an ordinary day. But even if we hypothetically assumed that the seventh day was a long age rather than an ordinary day, the age of the universe would still be constrained to about 6,000 years. Remember, Adam was made on the sixth day of creation, not the seventh (Genesis 1:26-31). And it is from the genealogies in Genesis 5 (and elsewhere) that we know the timespan between Adam and Abraham was about 2,000 years. So, in terms of computing the age of the universe, the length of the seventh day is not actually relevant. Six days before Adam, plus ~2,000 years between Adam and Abraham, plus ~4,000 years between Abraham and today yields ~6,000 years.

❖

The sun does not (primarily) determine the length of the day—the rotation of the earth fulfills that role.

❖

The claim (that the seventh day may not be an ordinary day since the text does not list an "evening" and "morning" with it) is actually tacit admission that the first six days are indeed ordinary days, since the text does specify an evening and morning with them. It shows that the critic of biblical creation really does know what the Bible is teaching—the seventh day is a day of rest, not a day of creation. So it is listed in a slightly different way. But it still has a number with it, and therefore, must be an ordinary day.

Some have said, "But the sun wasn't made until the fourth day. So how could the days be ordinary?" This objection comes from a basic misunderstanding of astronomy. The sun does not (primarily) determine the length of the day—the rotation of the earth fulfills that role. The sun simply provides a relatively permanent source of light; then, as the earth rotates on its axis, we experience morning and evening. As long as we have a rotating planet and a source of light, there will be ordinary days.

Was there light before the sun? Yes! Genesis 1:3 states, "Then God said, 'Let there be light;' and there was light." God provided a temporary source of light for the first three days, and then made the sun on the fourth day as a permanent light-bearer. The earth was already rotating the first three days; we know this because there was "evening" and "morning." All the days of creation would have been approximately 24 hours in length.

As a last-ditch effort, some might make the following claim: "Since God's ways are not our ways (Isaiah 55:8), perhaps His days are not our days. So when God speaks of 'days,' it doesn't mean the same thing as when man speaks of days." I have actually heard someone use this argument. But it is quite absurd. If words meant different things to different people, then communication would be impossible, and language would be useless! If words do not have a common meaning between speaker and listener, between writer and reader, then no ideas could ever be communicated. In such a case, reading the Bible would be pointless because when God says, "Turn and live" (Ezekiel 18:32), for all we know He might actually mean, "Put brussel sprouts in your ears."

Even if we made the days of creation into long ages, the order of events would not line up between the Bible and the secular/evolutionary timeline.

Order of Events

Christians who believe they can reconcile the Bible to the secular timeline by assuming the days of creation were long ages often overlook a very important inconsistency—the order of events. Even if we made the days of creation into long ages, the order of events would not line up between the Bible and the secular/evolutionary timeline.

◆ The Bible teaches that the earth was made on Day One, and the stars were made on Day Four. But the secular timeline has this reversed; the secularists believe that stars existed billions of years before the earth.

◆ The Bible teaches that fruit trees are made on Day Three, and then fish on Day Five. But the evolutionary timeline has fish evolving long before fruit trees (fish are found in deeper layers of rock strata than fruit trees).

◆ The Bible teaches that birds were created on Day Five, and all the land animals were made on Day Six (this would include things like dinosaurs, since they are land animals). However, the secular timescale has dinosaurs evolving long before birds.

A Gap?

There isn't any legitimate exegetical reason to believe that the days in Genesis were anything but ordinary 24-hour days. And yet some Christians feel that they must accept the (secular) idea of billions of years. So some Christians have suggested that although the days of creation were ordinary days, there was an enormous gap of time before Day One. They see the creation week as more of a re-creation week. Some in this camp believe that God originally made the world billions of years ago, and then it was ruined, perhaps by Satan, so that the creation days of Genesis reflect God (re)making the world in six ordinary days. This view is sometimes called "the gap theory," because advocates believe that an enormous gap of time (billions of years) lies between the first two verses of Genesis 1.

> ❖
>
> *Hebrew grammatical construction makes it impossible for a gap of time to exist between verses one and two.*
>
> ❖

"In the beginning God created the heavens and the earth" (Genesis 1:1). Gap theorists believe that this verse refers to the original creation billions of years ago. "The earth was without form, and void…" (Genesis 1:2). Gap theorists would like to translate verse two as "And the earth *became* without form and void." They see this verse as happening billions of years later, after an unrecorded history with lots of death and suffering.

There is no legitimate basis for a "gap" of time between verses one and two. And there is no basis for translating "was" as "became." In fact, Hebrew grammatical construction makes it impossible for a gap of time to exist between verses one and two. Why?

Genesis 1 makes frequent use of the *vav* consecutive, which is characterized by the word "and" followed by an action verb. Examples include "And God said...And God made." In Hebrew, the verb comes first, as in, "And said God... and made God." Consecutive events are clearly described in this construction. Genesis 1:2 is the one exception to the sentence structure. It is not *vav* consecutive; instead, it is a *vav* disjunctive, where "and" is followed by a noun in the Hebrew order. (In English, we see this most vividly in the King James Version.) So, where verse two states, "And the earth," we know that this is a *vav* disjunctive. Unlike the *vav* consecutive, the *vav* disjunctive does not indicate a sequence of events; rather, it indicates that verse two is a comment about verse one. An *explanation*.

Genesis 1:2 is a comment about how the earth looked when it was first created. The *vav* disjunctive here is a point of clarification, much like we use in a parenthetical comment, such as, "In the beginning God created the heavens and the earth (and the earth was without form and void)." The gap theory has been thoroughly refuted and is therefore not commonly espoused today.

Exodus 20:11

The gap theory, the Day-Age theory, and other hybrid theories of origins seek to insert billions of years into biblical creation, forcing an unnatural reading of Genesis that is untrue to the intentions of the author and inconsistent with other Scriptures. But God, the Author of the Bible, never leaves His Word without a clear defense. Consider Exodus 20:11.

❖

The fact that almost all cultures on earth have a seven- day week is evidence that they all originally knew about creation.

❖

For in six days the LORD made the heavens and the earth, the sea, and all that is in them, and rested the seventh day. Therefore the LORD blessed the Sabbath day and hallowed it.

The phrase "in six days" indicates a timespan. So, everything in heaven and earth (which is truly everything God made) was made by God in the span of six days.

A few verses before this passage, we find the Fourth Commandment: "Remember the Sabbath day, to keep it holy" (Exodus 20:8). And the pattern God established? "Six days you shall labor and do all your work" (verse nine). We are allowed to work six days a week, and then we are to take a day of rest according to the Fourth Commandment. Verse 11 explains why—we work six days and rest one because God created the universe in six days and rested one. So, if God had actually created over millions of years, we would have a very, very long week!

Clearly, we are to understand from Exodus 20:8-11 that our work week is based on the creation week. And the fact that almost all cultures on earth have a seven-day week is evidence that they all originally knew about creation.

Further, Exodus 20:11 does not allow for a previous creation or things that were made billions of years ago. The heaven, the earth, the sea, and *everything within them* were all made in the span of six ordinary days. The phrase "heaven and earth" is a merism—a figure of speech in which two opposite extremes are stated as a substitution for everything that lies between them as well, such as, "I looked high and low for the TV remote, but couldn't find it." By "high and low," we state two extremes as an idiom to include everything in between. We don't mean just literally high and literally low, but everywhere in between, too. Exodus 20:11 also includes the sea, lest someone be tempted to think that "earth" refers to the land only (which sometimes it does). The verse explicitly states "and all that is in them," as if to emphasize that God really is talking about absolutely everything!

Scientific evidence confirms that the universe is thousands of years old—not millions or billions.

Scientific evidence confirms that the universe is thousands of years old—not millions or billions (see the book *Thousands... Not Billions* by Don DeYoung). In our evolution-saturated science and education system, this evidence is not widely discussed because the data and conclusions run counter to the prevailing belief of a very old earth. What are some of these evidences?

Ordinary carbon is called C-12; the number 12 indicates the atomic mass, the number of protons plus neutrons in the nucleus. There is a less common variety of carbon called C-14 that has two extra neutrons. Unlike C-12, C-14 is unstable—it will spontaneously change (decay) into nitrogen on a timescale of about 5,700 years. This timescale is called the "half life," because if you had a chunk of solid C-14, half of it will have decayed into nitrogen in a span of 5,700 years. C-14 certainly cannot last even one million years, because not a single atom would be left. So it came as quite a surprise (for evolutionists) to find C-14 in just about everything in the fossil record that has carbon in it. We even found C-14 in diamonds that are supposed to be billions of years old (by secular thinking). But obviously they cannot be even one million years old or there would be no C-14 left! Evolutionists and other old-earth advocates must have blind faith that there is some sort of as-yet-undiscovered contamination of the source material, even though nothing like that has been detected.

Radiometric dating allegedly proves that rocks are billions of years old. Such methods make use of the fact that rocks contain traces of radioactive materials like Uranium-238, which decays into lead via a chain of other elements on a very slow timescale—much slower than C-14. By comparing the ratio of elements and making certain assumptions, scientists try to estimate when the rock first formed. What you may not have heard is that such methods also "prove" that brand new rocks are also millions of years old! Yes, rocks that have been formed recently (a few years ago) in volcanoes have also been "dated" by radiometric methods and found to be hundreds of thousands to millions of years old!

But they are not that old because *we observed their formation.* This strongly implies that other rocks that have been age-dated at millions of years are also much, much younger. Many other lines of evidence could be presented (and have been presented in other resources) that show the age of the earth to be consistent with the biblical timescale.

WHY TIME MATTERS

The major Christian doctrines have their foundation in the literal historical account of Genesis. Things such as marriage, the sanctity of life, and even the gospel message would be absurd apart from biblical creation. But what about the timescale of creation? We have seen that the Bible unquestionably teaches creation in six ordinary days, a few thousand years ago. But does it really matter? If a Christian believes in creation, but also believes it took millions of years, is that really such a big deal?

We have seen that the Bible unquestionably teaches creation in six ordinary days, a few thousand years ago.

Some Christians have the attitude that the timescale is not really important as long as we don't believe in evolution. Some might actually believe in a six-day creation, but they don't like to bring this up in conversations because it might be a stumbling block to people.

They often express some version of the following sentiments: "When we're witnessing, let's avoid the topic of six days. After all, most people believe in billions of years. Why take on an additional argument that is not really that important? It's not a salvation issue, after all. We need to choose our battles. So let's focus on teaching them about salvation in Christ, and then maybe later we can deal with minor matters like the timescale of creation."

Sounds pretty reasonable, doesn't it?

Is Creation a Salvation Issue?

The timescale of creation is far more important than most people think. But can a person be saved (redeemed by God's grace through faith in Christ) without accepting that God made the universe in six days? The Bible is clear—belief in six days of creation is not a prerequisite for salvation. Yes, of course, you can be saved without committing to the biblical timescale. But at the same time, that doesn't make the timescale an irrelevant side issue. Rejecting any portion of the Bible isn't acceptable.

> ❖
>
> *The Bible makes it abundantly clear that we are not saved by having absolute, perfect theology.*
>
> ❖

The Bible makes it abundantly clear that we are not saved by having absolute, perfect theology. We all err at times in our understanding and application of the Scriptures. But that (by itself) does not prevent the Lord from saving us. The Bible declares that we are saved by God's grace received through faith in Christ (Ephesians 2:8).

By way of analogy, consider the law of gravity. Belief in gravity is not a requirement for salvation. You can certainly go to heaven without believing in gravity. In fact, you will probably get there much sooner! But that doesn't make gravity an irrelevant issue. It is very important! If you reject the existence of gravity, you will shortly experience some very negative consequences as a result of your unbelief. And so it is with the biblical timescale. There are two reasons why the timescale of creation is an important issue.

A Matter of Inerrancy

First, the timescale of creation has implications upon the inerrancy of Scripture. Inerrancy is the belief that the Bible has no errors in the original writings. This would certainly make sense if the Bible really is inspired ("breathed") by God, as it claims to be (2 Timothy 3:16). The all-powerful, all-knowing God certainly does not make mistakes. Jesus indicates that every word of God (Matthew 4:4), even the smallest letter (*jot*) and even the smallest part of the smallest letter (*tittle*), is absolutely authoritative and will outlast heaven and earth (Matthew 5:18).

If the Bible is inerrant, then so is the timescale given in Genesis. We can have absolute confidence that God really did create the universe and Everything within it in six days. In fact, the section of Scripture that says "for in six days the LORD made the heavens and the earth" (Exodus 20:11) was actually written by the finger of God on stone at Mt. Sinai (Exodus 32:15-16). We had better take it seriously!

On the other hand, if God really did not create everything in six days, then Genesis 1 (as well as Exodus 20:11) is in error. And if such sections of the Bible are in error, then obviously the Bible is not inerrant. If there are mistakes in Genesis, then there might be mistakes in other places as well. If the Bible is wrong about six days, then how can we have any confidence in anything else it teaches?

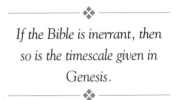

If the Bible is inerrant, then so is the timescale given in Genesis.

How can we be sure that other portions are not also in error?

Jesus put it like this, "If I have told you earthly things and you do not believe, how will you believe if I tell you heavenly things?" (John 3:12). If we cannot trust the Bible in matters of simple historical facts, then how can we possibly trust it in spiritual matters? Many Christians are tempted to believe in billions of years because they have confidence in what the secular scientists teach. But then again, Christians readily accept the resurrection of Christ, the virgin birth, Jesus turning water into wine, and so on—all of which are rejected by secular scientists.

Some might respond, "But those are miraculous events—the miracles of Christ go beyond natural law. Normal scientific procedure would not apply." But isn't creation a miraculous event? God spoke the universe into existence—something He does not do today. Creation goes beyond the normal everyday operation of the universe. If we arbitrarily dismiss the possibility of supernatural action by God in Genesis, then to be logically consistent, we would have to reject the other miracles in Scripture as well, including the resurrection of Christ—and the resurrection is indeed a "salvation issue" (1 Corinthians 15:14, 17).

If we were to follow the line of thinking that rejects the six-day biblical account of creation to its inevitable conclusion, we would see that, although belief in a six-day creation is not necessary for salvation, a rejection of six days inexorably leads to a rejection of the resurrection.

Sin and Death

Second, the timescale of creation explains the occurrence of death as the judgment for sin. And we can see this on display in fossils we find all over the world. A fossil is the preserved remains of an organism, such as animal bones that have turned to stone (although there are other types of fossils as well). A fossil of this kind is created when an animal dies and is rapidly buried. The soft parts of the animal usually decay, but the bones mineralize. This means that minerals move into the bones, filling up all the holes and making the bone much heavier than it was originally. We end up with a rock that is in the shape of the original bone.

But if death was already in existence before Adam sinned, then how can death be the result of Adam's sin?

Evolutionary scientists usually believe that fossils are many millions of years old, depending on where they are found in rock strata. But this presents an enormous theological problem. A fossil is evidence of death. So if fossils are millions of years old, then there was death *before* Adam sinned. After all, everyone agrees that human beings were not around millions of years ago. But if death was already in existence before Adam sinned, then how can death be the result of Adam's sin?

The Bible teaches that death was the result of Adam's sin. Sin entered the world through Adam, and death entered through that sin (Romans 5:12; 1 Corinthians 15:21). This fact is foundational to the gospel. Because "the wages of sin is death" (Romans 6:23), it was necessary for Christ to die on the cross to pay for our sins. But if the world already had death in it, then how can death be the wages of sin? Would it make sense to say "by man came death" (1 Corinthians 15:21) if death were already in the world millions of years before man? How could death be the penalty for sin if it preceded sin by millions of years? And if death is not the penalty for sin, then how could we make sense of the gospel?

Not only are fossils evidence of death, but some fossils also contain evidence of disease. Scientists have found evidence of arthritis, cancer, and other diseases in fossils that evolutionists believe to be millions of years old. But doesn't the Bible describe the original creation as a paradise—a world that God called "very good" (Genesis 1:31)? Some people mistakenly think that only the Garden of Eden was a paradise and that the rest of the world was not. But Genesis 1:31 indicates that *everything* was very good—not just the Garden of Eden. Would a "very good" world have been full of disease? If you accept the secular belief that fossils are millions of years old, then God's very good world was full of death and suffering.

The Bible teaches that death came about as the result of Adam's sin. It follows therefore that fossils are not millions of years old; rather, they formed after Adam sinned. The worldwide Flood described in Genesis 6-8 would naturally account for the fossils we find on earth.

Not Just Human Death

Is it possible that only human death entered the world at the time of Adam's sin? Could animals have already been living and dying? The Bible makes that idea impossible to reconcile. Although passages like Romans 5:12 focus mainly on human death, other passages such as Romans 8:21-22 indicate that *all creation* was cursed when Adam sinned—not just humanity. Genesis 1:31 states that all creation was very good; this would certainly include the animals. So, when we find evidence of horrible disease in animal fossils and evidence of violence (one animal killing another), we can be confident that this was not part of the original "very good" creation. Rather, fossils show evidence of a fallen world—a world marred by the Curse of sin.

The Bible makes it clear that God instituted animal death when Adam and Eve sinned. The clothing that God provided for Adam and Eve was not made from plants. God gave them animal skin. God killed an animal (or animals) in response to sin. Animal death began at the Fall.

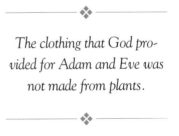

The clothing that God provided for Adam and Eve was not made from plants.

What about plant death? Could plants die in a perfect world? We know from Genesis that Adam and Eve (and the living creatures) were given plants for food (Genesis 1:29-30). So plants, or at least parts of plants, would have "died" before Adam sinned. Does this mean death really was in the world before sin?

The Bible never refers to plants as "alive." Scripture uses a particular Hebrew word (*nephesh*) to indicate life. This word is used to describe people and animals, but it is never used to describe plants. According to the biblical taxonomy, plants are not truly alive and, therefore, do not really "die."

Describing a dead tree is a figurative use of the word "dead," since a tree was never truly alive, at least not in the same way that we are. Likewise, a dead battery never lived like humans live.

Modern biologists define life differently than the biblical text. They include plants as well as microbes in the group of living things, and there is nothing wrong with classifying them that way. But we understand that a tree is not alive *in the same way* as an animal. You might sit on a dead tree in the woods, but would you sit on a dead animal in the woods? We understand that there is a qualitative difference between plant "life" and animals that are truly alive. Living (*nephesh*) creatures did not experience death before sin.

Some have erroneously claimed that death (of living creatures) is a necessary part of creation. But from a Christian perspective, it is irrational to think that an all-powerful God could not design life without the need for death. The Bible teaches that, in the future, death will be destroyed (1 Corinthians 15:26; Revelation 20:14). There will certainly be no death in heaven— another indicator that death is not necessary for life.

Critics might say, "What about overpopulation? And some animals only eat meat. So there must have been death before Adam sinned." But such reasoning is an irrational extrapolation based on today's cursed world. Today some animals eat meat, but originally they were all vegetarian (Genesis 1:30). Overpopulation of animals in some regions is a problem, but before the Curse, God would have maintained the world in perfect balance. It seems reasonable that God would have caused animals to slow or stop their rate of reproduction as they approached filling their environmental niche.

The timescale of creation does matter because it is crucial to inerrancy and to the gospel. If the Bible cannot be trusted about the six days of creation, then where does the truth begin? If the Bible really is the Word of God, then would it really make sense to think that it could contain errors? Does God make mistakes? He ought to know how He made the universe.

Furthermore, compromising on the timescale of creation undermines the gospel message. If fossils are millions of years old, then death cannot be the penalty for sin. So why did God send His Son to die a horrible death on a cross? The gospel message is logically connected to the literal history recorded in Genesis.

5

BEGIN AT THE BEGINNING

Christians are rightly concerned about the condition of the world today. There are literally billions of people in today's world who do not know the Lord. These people are perishing in their sin, headed toward a miserable eternity of separation from the loving presence of God. Christians have a duty and a strong desire to reach these people with the gospel message. And many Christians do.

We witness to our friends and others that we meet. We send missionaries to foreign lands to spread the Good News to all of creation. And yet, for all this evangelism, there are still billions of non-Christians in the world. Why? Some of this can be attributed to the fact that we are still not doing enough. We need more missionaries, and we need to do more to share the Word of God with our unbelieving friends.

Yet, it still seems that we are missing a crucial piece of the puzzle.

Perhaps most perplexing of all is the number of non-Christians in the United States. This nation was founded primarily by Christians and based on Christian ideals. And yet Christianity seems to be on the decline in terms of the socio-political

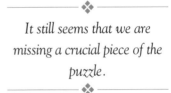

It still seems that we are missing a crucial piece of the puzzle.

climate. There are millions of sincere Christians in the United States and more Christian resources (bookstores, radio stations, television programs) than in any other nation. So, how can Christianity be on the decline in this nation? And why has the church not been successful (so far) in evangelizing the world?

The teaching of evolution has certainly had its influence. Evolution undermines the credibility of the Bible from its foundation in Genesis. Just as Jesus said to Nicodemus, "If I have told you earthly things and you do not believe, how will you believe if I tell you heavenly things?" (John 3:12). People have been taught that the Bible cannot be trusted at its foundation in Genesis; so they have little reason to trust the gospel message that stems from that foundation. I suggest that one of the main reasons the church has not been as effective as it could be is because most Christians have not been faithful in the area of apologetics (the defense of the faith). The church has compromised God's Word rather than defending it.

> ❖
>
> *People have been taught that the Bible cannot be trusted at its foundation in Genesis; so they have little reason to trust the gospel message that stems from that foundation.*
>
> ❖

The Lord knew that there would be opposition to the gospel message. It is the nature of unbelievers to reject the truth, particularly in areas that would call them to be accountable to God. Therefore, the Lord instructed us to be ready at all times to give an answer—a rational defense of the faith—to anyone who asks, and to do so respectfully (1 Peter 3:15).

This is what we call "apologetics." We are supposed to refute ("cast down") any argument or speculation that is contrary to the Word of God (2 Corinthians 10:5). We need to study the issues so that we can defend the Bible when critics come against it. And for the most part, Christians aren't prepared for this part of their ministry. Instead of standing on the authority of the Bible and defending its foundation in the historical record of Genesis, we have either ignored the topic of origins, or worse—we have compromised with the secular world. As a result, the church has been severely weakened in its effort to make disciples of all nations. Christians cannot effectively spread the Word of God if they 1) do not really believe all of it, or 2) do not know how to defend it.

Treat the Problem, Not the Symptom

We live in a symptom-driven society. When dealing with a particular difficulty, we tend to try to alleviate the symptom, rather than dealing with the underlying problem. Have a headache? Take an aspirin. But the headache isn't the problem; it's the symptom. Maybe the problem is that you are not getting enough sleep or you need a new prescription for your glasses. The point is that we want a quick fix rather than a lasting solution.

Likewise, the particular difficulties in our society (school violence, abortion, sexual perversion, crime, bad laws, economic failure, loss of freedom, and so on) are not really the main problems. They are symptoms of an underlying problem—the loss of biblical authority, beginning with Genesis.

And yet most Christians concentrate only on the symptoms of our societal ills, and they never deal with the actual problem. Many Christian programs try to alleviate school violence, abortion, drugs, and so on. And yet, few Christians study about how to defend Christianity, beginning with Genesis. By the way, there is nothing wrong with trying to alleviate symptoms; I am certainly not against Christian programs that try to deal with social issues like abortion, any more than I am against taking an aspirin for a headache. The point is that we must not limit our efforts merely to the symptoms. We must deal with the problem—the attack on God's Word, beginning in Genesis.

> ❖
>
> *Most Christians concentrate only on the symptoms of our societal ills, and they never deal with the actual problem.*
>
> ❖

The key to solving the issues of our world is to teach people that they can stand confidently on the authority of the Word of God. The Bible can be trusted on all matters that it touches. Christians must refute the fallacious arguments of the critics, show the scientific absurdity of evolution, demonstrate the philosophical bankruptcy of secular thinking, and defend the Bible from its foundation in Genesis. When people have legitimate questions about the Bible, we study and provide answers for them. When skeptics try to argue for their versions of origins, we respectfully point out the absurdity of such positions. Is there any doubt that the Lord would use this to bring millions upon millions of people to salvation? We could easily see the United States turn back to God if only Christians would do what the Lord has already told us to do.

Start at the Beginning

It's not by accident that the Bible starts in Genesis. Without Genesis, we really cannot make sense of any Christian doctrine.

Why have a Savior die on a cross if there is no Adam? What is sin if there was no fall of man? What is marriage if there were no Adam and Eve? The Bible gave us the foundational history in Genesis so that we could understand the basis for Christian principles. But since that history has been attacked so much in our culture today, people are increasingly rejecting the Christian principles that stem from Genesis. It's not surprising that we see an increasing number of people attempting to redefine marriage or to keep God out of public life. If we are to reverse such moral decay, we must begin in Genesis.

When I see many Christians attempting to defend their faith, I am sometimes reminded of the television game show *Jeopardy*. This show reverses the normal trivia challenge by providing its players with an answer for which they are supposed to figure out the question. Each player must respond with a phrase like "What is _____?" or "Who is _____?" It's a backwards type of game—and so is the average Christian's approach to evangelism. Christians say things like, "Jesus is the Answer!" But the world responds, "What was the question?"

❖

Christianity makes sense in light of a literal Genesis; it makes no sense to evolutionists.

❖

Christianity makes sense in light of a literal Genesis; it makes no sense to evolutionists. But most unbelievers have not been taught Genesis. They believe in some form of evolution, which is the wrong foundation for the gospel message. It does little good to tell people about the gospel (the "good news") if they don't understand the bad news (that mankind is lost because of Adam's sin).

What happens when we don't begin in Genesis? Let's consider one example. When unbelievers hear "Trust in Jesus to be saved," it is all too common for them to respond with "Saved from what? I'm doing just fine. And who is Jesus anyway? Wasn't he an ancient prophet/teacher? Why trust Him as opposed to any other ancient prophet—Buddha or Mohammed?"

The Christian says, "Believe in Jesus, and you will go to heaven when you die." The non-believer responds, "Why should I believe that? I'm basically a good person. I haven't murdered anybody, and I don't cheat on my wife. So I think God will let me into heaven. And hasn't science disproved the Bible, anyway?"

These types of responses are all too common in a society that does not have an adequate understanding of God as Creator. God is perfectly holy and just, and sin is high treason against the King of kings. But God wouldn't be holy if He let treason go unpunished. And Genesis teaches us that one sin is sufficient to alienate us from perfect fellowship with our Creator. That sin doesn't have to be murder or adultery. All Adam did was eat from a tree. But this action was nonetheless *treason* because it was contrary to God's command. It warranted the death penalty. The beauty of the gospel is that God took our penalty upon Himself and has provided freedom from the Curse of sin to all who will trust in Him. This is the full gospel message; it's a message that God first revealed in Genesis.

Greeks and Jews

The Jews living at the time of Jesus' earthly ministry understood Genesis, and so they knew they needed a Savior. But most of them did not realize that Jesus was that Savior. The fact that Jesus is the promised Savior was a "stumbling block" for them. On the other hand, the Greeks at the time of Christ had no knowledge of Genesis, for the most part. They believed in a very old earth and universe and had no concept of original sin or the curse. In fact, their beliefs were similar in many ways to the beliefs of evolutionists today. So the Greeks were not expecting a Savior. They didn't realize they needed one. To them, the gospel message was utter nonsense. The Bible explains this in 1 Corinthians 1:23: "But we preach Christ crucified, to the Jews a stumbling block and to the Greeks foolishness."

The Greeks were not expecting a Savior.

In Acts 2:14-41, we read an account in which the apostle Peter preaches a message to the unbelieving Jews. Peter understood that these Jews knew about Genesis. They knew about original sin. They knew that the penalty for sin is death and that we all deserve death and separation from God's love. They knew about the promised Savior, who would deliver them from their sins. Thus, Peter reasoned with them from the Scriptures to show them that Jesus is indeed the promised Savior. All Peter had to do was to help them over that stumbling block.

On the other hand, in Acts 17:18-34, we read of Paul preaching to the Greek philosophers on Mars Hill. The Greeks did not have any of the foundational knowledge of Genesis. Instead, they had an incorrect foundation of an evolutionary type of philosophy. And Paul was aware of this.

So he began with Genesis.

Paul explained the nature of God to his listeners by pointing out that God is the Creator of heaven and earth (Acts 17:24) and that God has been sovereign over human history. He refers to the fact that we are all descended from one man (Acts 17:26). Not only did Paul present what Genesis teaches, He refuted the Greek alternative. He showed them that the Greek gods are nothing of the kind; they are placed in a temple made by people and cannot possibly create or control the world (Acts 17:24-25). He demonstrated the inconsistency and arbitrariness in their thinking, and replaced their faulty view of origins with the true history of Genesis. Only after this groundwork had been laid did Paul move on and talk about repentance and, finally, the resurrection of Christ (Acts 17:30-31).

Paul's strategy with these erudite, intellectual Greeks was to knock down their faulty worldview and replace it with the truth about the Creator.

Curiously, some Christians have taken away the wrong message from Acts 17:18-34. They say that Paul's message really wasn't very effective; after all, only a few people got saved. They say that Peter was far more effective in Acts 2, since 3,000 people were saved. They conclude therefore that all our messages should be like Peter's and not like Paul's. But doesn't this overlook something rather significant?

> ❖
>
> *They need to have their faulty, evolutionary worldview exposed and the foundational knowledge of Genesis revealed so that they also may come to an understanding of the gospel.*
>
> ❖

Paul was preaching to people who were *hostile to the Bible and rejected Genesis*, whereas Peter was preaching to Jews who readily embraced the Scriptures! Paul had a much tougher crowd, and it would be unreasonable to expect as many to be saved given those circumstances, and especially in light of what the Bible teaches in 1 Corinthians 1:23.

Paul was very successful, but not everyone responded positively to his message. Some sneered, but others wanted to hear more (Acts 17:32). And most impressively, some people embraced the message and believed right away (Acts 17:34). Considering the difficult audience, Paul was very successful indeed.

Consider this: Is today's world more like the Jews of Acts 2 or the Greeks of Acts 17? Do most people believe in the history of Genesis, or do they believe in some alternative like evolution? Clearly, our world today is more like the Greeks. Now consider this: what type of messages do we hear primarily today? What were the last five messages you heard at church? Did they teach you how to refute non-biblical worldviews or show how the history in Genesis connects to Christian doctrines? Did they equip you to defend your faith with confidence, to cast down anti-Christian arguments, and to share your faith with "Greeks" who have no knowledge of the Creator God? If they did, you are part of a very good but rare church body.

Evangelism can take many forms, and there is certainly nothing wrong with preaching Acts 2-type sermons. Some people need to hear that. Some people already do believe in creation, have some knowledge of sin, and recognize that they need a Savior. These are like the Jews, and we should preach the gospel like Peter did in Acts 2. But we must also recognize that many people in our world need a message like Paul preached to the Greeks on Mars Hill. They need to have their faulty, evolutionary worldview exposed and the foundational knowledge of Genesis revealed so that they also may come to an understanding of the gospel. Especially in our post modern society we have to do some apologetics in order for our evangelism to be effective.

In the past, this was not as much of an issue as it is today. The United States of America was established primarily by Christians. Consequently, for most of its

❖

We are more and more a culture similar to the skeptical Greeks of Paul's day.

❖

history this nation has enjoyed a cultural heritage that is (for the most part) Christian. Most Americans attended church regularly and professed the Christian worldview. Even those who were not Christians were influenced by Christianity and often had respect for the Bible and biblical principles. Most people believed in biblical creation. It would be fair to say that in the past, the United States had a culture that was more like the Jews of Acts 2 than the Greeks of Acts 17.

In the past, the church could more readily preach "Christ crucified." And since most people believed in creation and had some knowledge of the Bible, the preaching of the gospel was effective in helping unbelievers over that "stumbling block." Even in the 20th century, we saw many millions of people come to salvation through evangelistic crusades all over the world. Acts 2 messages are highly effective with an Acts 2 audience.

And that's the point. All of us must be mindful of who we are reaching with our teaching and evangelism.

Today, our culture has become much more like the Greeks of Acts 17. Many reject Genesis and embrace evolution as the explanation of origins. Many of these people simply won't bother to listen to an Acts 2 sermon. They want proof. They need our ministry of apologetics (1 Peter 3:15), often as a bridge to evangelism. Recognizing our modern audience—that we are more and more a culture similar to the skeptical Greeks of Paul's day—will help all of us communicate the gospel in terms these skeptics can understand.

Paul's sermon in Acts 17 is a superb example for us to follow, expounding the gospel from its start in Genesis to the "Greeks" of our day. We must be ready to cast down every argument that dares to challenge God's Word, communicating boldly in a manner that resonates with our modern-day "Greek" culture. Following biblical patterns of teaching will no doubt result in many more millions responding to the message of the gospel, acknowledging God the Creator as Lord and Savior and King.

WHY GENESIS MATTERS

The book of Genesis is not simply a collection of moral stories or fables about our origins. It's a book that sets the foundation for the whole of Scripture and upon which all the other books of the Bible rest. Genesis is essential to understanding God our Creator, Judge, and Savior. Every vital Christian doctrine finds its roots in the Genesis record. And so we must be careful to hold this first book of the Bible in the same regard as Deuteronomy or 1 Kings or Psalms or the gospels.

Genesis matters because it is inspired revelation from God. The Author of the Bible began His revelation with Genesis and finished with Revelation. We must not disparage the sacred nature of Genesis.

Genesis matters because it is accurate historical narrative. The Hebrew grammar, vocabulary, structure, and context clearly define the text of Genesis as recorded history. There is no place for interpreting Genesis as symbolic musings of a confused God. The text of Genesis won't allow sloppy interpretation, nor will the rest of Scripture.

Genesis matters because it is vital to knowing God. You cannot truly know God unless you rightly understand Genesis. God intended mankind to know Him as the One who in the beginning created the heavens and the earth. The unique-

Genesis is essential to understanding God our Creator, Judge, and Savior.

ness of life, fellowship with God, the pattern for marriage, the entrance of sin, the consequence of death, and the judgment of God are all features of Genesis that point every human being toward a knowledge of God, and in our understanding of the Creator, we come to know our Savior.

And Genesis, it seems, matters more today because our culture is bent on excluding God from every thought and every place in our mortal lives. Governments denounce God. Schools avoid God. Secular science mocks God. And more and more churches are denigrating the character of the Creator by denouncing the fact of recent creation as described in Genesis. Pastors are abdicating the Genesis message by embracing liberal scholars who declare that Adam and Eve were not real people, that the Fall was simply symbolic, and that the Flood of Noah's day was nothing more than a local splash of water in ancient Mesopotamia.

Now is the time for God's people to do the hard work of biblical apologetics, embracing the full message of the Bible, beginning in Genesis, in order to rightly defend the Scriptures and compassionately persuade men, that some might be saved.

ENDNOTES

1. Microorganisms and plants are not classified as "living" in the biblical taxonomic system. The Hebrew language uses a specific phrase (*nephesh chayah*) to refer to living creatures—animals and human beings. This phrase is never applied to plants.

2. Well, there are some people who force their pets to wear ridiculous outfits. But this is an example of personification—giving human traits to a non-person. It's not intrinsic to the animal, which is why it often strikes us as being comical.

Jason Lisle, Ph.D.

As Director of Research, Dr. Lisle leads ICR's gifted team of scientists who continue to investigate and demonstrate the evidence for creation. He graduated *summa cum laude* from Ohio Wesleyan University, where he double-majored in physics and astronomy and minored in mathematics. He earned a master's degree and a Ph.D. in astrophysics at the University of Colorado. Dr. Lisle specialized in solar astrophysics, and has made a number of scientific discoveries regarding the solar photosphere and has contributed to the field of general relativity. After completion of his research at the University of Colorado, Dr. Lisle began working in full-time apologetics ministry, focusing on the defense of Genesis. Dr. Lisle was instrumental in developing the planetarium at the Creation Museum in Kentucky, writing and directing popular planetarium shows, including "The Created Cosmos." Dr. Lisle speaks on topics relating to science and the defense of the Christian faith using logic and correct reasoning; he has authored numerous articles and books demonstrating that biblical creation is the only logical possibility for origins.

Jason Lisle's books include:
- *The Ultimate Proof of Creation*
- *Discerning Truth: Exposing Errors in Evolutionary Arguments*
- *Stargazer's Guide to the Night Sky*
- *Taking Back Astronomy*
- *A Pocket Guide to Logic & Faith*

THE BOOK OF BEGINNINGS:

A Practical Guide to Understand and Teach Genesis

VOLUME ONE:
Creation, Fall, and the First Age

Commentaries on Genesis today range from the fanciful to the technical. The book of beginnings has been debated for centuries by theologians, linguists, and scientists.

Why should you take the trouble to read another book on Genesis?

Perhaps the best reason is *urgency*. Over the past four generations, Christianity has precipitated from a large majority belief system among those who came of age during the first half of the 20th century to something less than 15 percent of young adults entering educational institutions and the workforce today.

If you are considering this book, you are probably bothered by these conditions and are looking for ways to help those in your sphere of influence find their way out of the morass.

In *The Book of Beginnings*, Dr. Henry Morris III addresses the tough issues in the Genesis record in a way that will not only give you confidence in your study of the Scriptures, but also as you communicate the richness of Genesis to those around you.

To order, call **800.628.7640**, or visit **www.icr.org/store**

FOR MORE INFORMATION

Sign up for ICR's FREE publications!

Our monthly *Acts & Facts* magazine offers fascinating articles and current information on creation, evolution, and more. Our quarterly *Days of Praise* booklet provides daily devotionals—real biblical "meat"— to strengthen and encourage the Christian witness.

To subscribe, call **800.337.0375** or mail your address information to the address below. Or sign up online at **www.icr.org**.

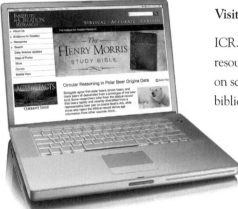

Visit ICR Online

ICR.org offers a wealth of resources and information on scientific creationism and biblical worldview issues.

- Read our news postings on today's hottest science topics
- Explore the evidence for creation
- Investigate our graduate and professional education programs
- Dive into our archive of 40 years of scientific articles
- Listen to current and past radio programs
- Watch our *That's a Fact* video show
- Explore our *Science Essentials* education resources
- And more!

Visit our online store at **www.icr.org/store** for more great resources.

INSTITUTE FOR CREATION RESEARCH

P. O. Box 59029
Dallas, TX 75229
800.337.0375

WHO'S RIGHT?

There's a better way to solve the evolution question.

Join the conversation.

www.youroriginsmatter.com